SOCIAL SCIENCE PRIMARY 6

BY ME

ACTIVITY BOOK

PABLO HERRANZ

UNIT 1 Planet Earth

① What do you know about the Solar System? Write two facts about each of the words.

The Moon

1. ______________________

2. ______________________

The Earth

1. ______________________

2. ______________________

Mars

1. ______________________

2. ______________________

Revolution

1. ______________________

2. ______________________

② Match the photos of severe weather to their names. Write the correct numbers in the boxes.

1

2

3

4

5

6

flood ☐

tornado ☐

lightning ☐

hailstorm ☐

wildfire ☐

tropical cyclone ☐

3 Rewrite the sentences about the Earth and the Moon correctly.

1. The Earth is tilted towards the Sun in winter.

___

2. It takes the Moon 45 days to complete one revolution.

___

3. The Earth revolves on its axis.

___

4. The Earth is the closest planet to the Sun.

___

4 Explain why life cannot exist on the Moon.

___

___

___

5 Complete the text about the Moon. Use the words from the box. There are some extra words.

light	Earth's	days	stars	phases	
receives	planets	position	reflects	shape	Sun

The moon is the ________ only natural satellite. The Moon orbits our planet in twenty-eight ________. It also takes the same time to complete one rotation. Therefore, we always see the same side of the Moon from the Earth. The Moon does not produce its own ________. It ________ light from the Sun and ________ some sunlight to the Earth. Obviously, we can only see the illuminated part that is facing the Earth. This is why, when we look at the Moon on different nights during the lunar month, its ________ changes. These different shapes are called the ________ of the Moon.

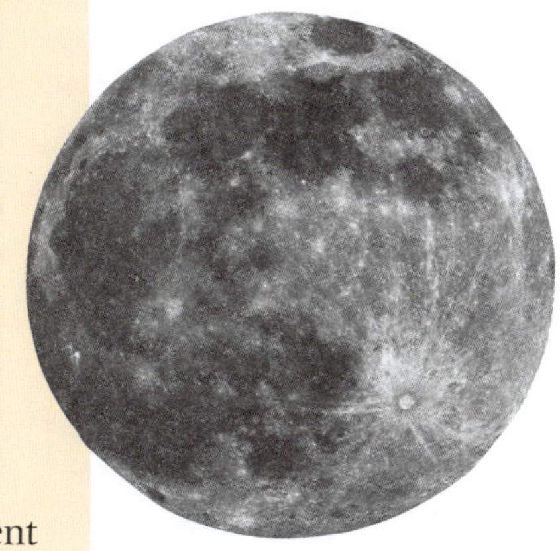

6. Label the picture with the words from the box.

outer layer	exosphere	500 km	thermosphere	ozone layer	50 km
mesosphere	12 km	weather	80 km	auroras	stratosphere
closest layer to the Earth	troposphere	10 000 km	coldest layer		

7. Read the sentences. Identify whether they refer to the geosphere (G) or the hydrosphere (H).

a. It is the solid and rigid part of the Earth. ☐

b. It contains all bodies of water. ☐

c. The crust forms the mountains. ☐

d. It covers 70 per cent of the Earth. ☐

8. What's the difference between each pair of words?

a. river / lake

b. glacier / iceberg

9. Think of rivers and lakes in your country. Write some examples.

Rivers:

Lakes:

10. Answer the questions about the water cycle.

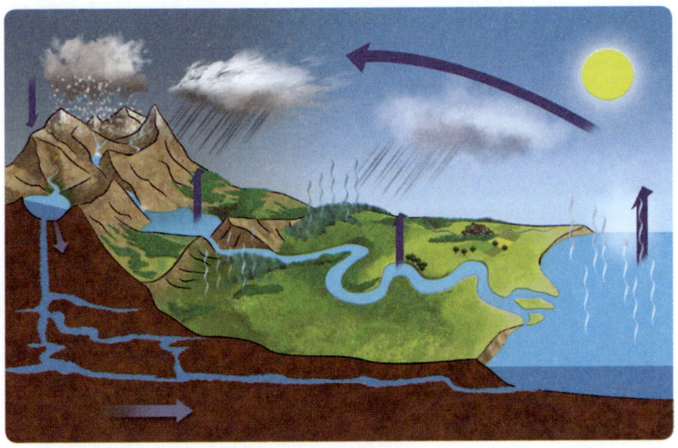

1. What forms can precipitation take?

rain,

2. What does the Earth do with water until it is needed?

3. What happens when the Sun comes out and heats up the water?

4. What are formed when vapour in the air gets cold and turns back into liquid?

Project work

11 Look at these coordinates and identify the cities on the map below.

1. 59° N, 10° E **2.** 26° S, 28ª E **3.** 52° N, 21ª E **4.** 40° N, 74° W

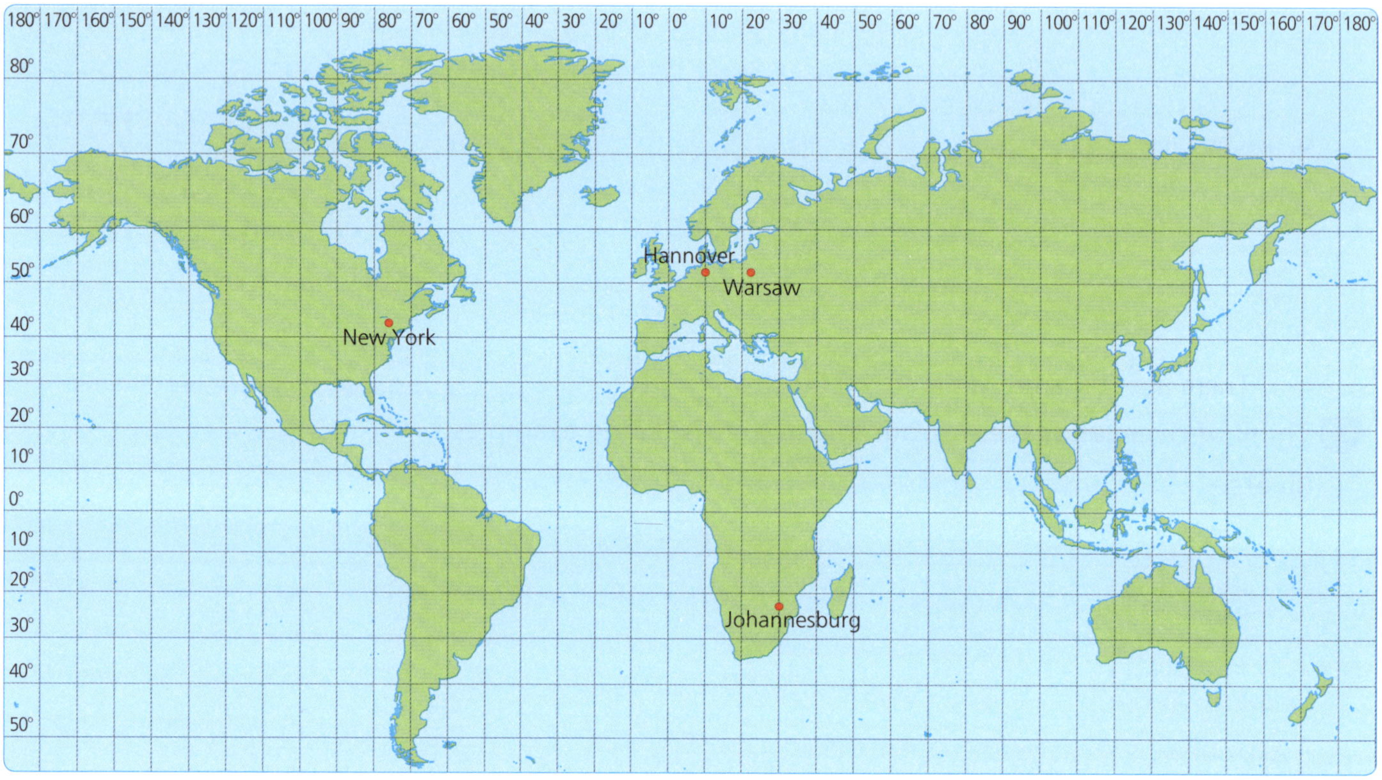

12 Complete the table with information about the cities above. Search for the information on the Internet.

city	coordinates	country and continent	climate	inhabitants

13 Locate the following cities on the map and write their coordinates.

a. Caracas: ______ **b.** Cairo: ______ **c.** Lima: ______ **d.** Costa Rica: ______

Skills check

14 Complete the second sentences so that they mean the same as the first ones.

1. a. The Earth is relatively close to Venus.

b. The Earth isn't ______________________________ Venus.

2. a. The environment on Earth is better for you than the one on Mars.

b. Mars isn't ______________________________ you as the Earth.

3. a. Stars can be seen using a telescope.

b. You ______________________________ using a telescope.

4. a. There are only a few different bodies of water on Earth.

b. There aren't ______________________________ bodies of water on Earth.

5. a. If you want to learn more about the Earth, you need to do more research.

b. You'll learn more about the Earth ______________________________ you do more research.

15 Complete the text using prepositions.

Astronauts will have to produce their own food if, ______________ the future, they stay ______________ the Moon ______________ long periods of time. Obviously, they won't plant the seeds on the Earth, but they will be ______________ special boxes which will contain the nutrients the plant needs, as well as water and air.

Once the garden lands ______________ the Moon, more water will be added. The scientists will study the germination ______________ the seeds.

UNIT 2 Geography of Spain

1 Read the sentences. Are they true (T) or false (F)?

	true	false
1. Spain is located in south-west Europe.	☐	☐
2. The Mediterranean Sea borders the whole of Spain.	☐	☐
3. Spain has five different climates.	☐	☐
4. The Meseta is in the south of the Iberian Peninsula.	☐	☐
5. There are 19 Autonomous Communities in Spain.	☐	☐

2 Read the texts and write the names of the Autonomous Community they refer to. Then, match them with their flags.

1. My hometown is in an Autonomous Community in western Spain and it is bordered by Portugal to the west. Our flag is green, white and black. The official language is Spanish. The area I live in has a lot of wildlife. The climate is Mediterranean.

   ____

2. My hometown is in an Autonomous Community in the north of Spain. Its capital is Logroño. Our flag is red, white, green and yellow. The official language is Spanish. The region is famous for its wine production. The climate is continental and alpine in some parts of the south.

   ____

3. My hometown is in an Autonomous Community in the south-east. It has been designated a 'historical nationality'. Our flag is made up of yellow and red lines with blue and yellow to the left. There are two official languages. The climate is generally Mediterranean.

   ____

3 Find out about the flag of the Comunidad de Madrid. What do the stars mean?

____

____

____

____

4 Look at the map and the photos. Then, answer the questions below.

1. What do the cities written on the map have in common?

____

2. Which Autonomous Community corresponds to each capital city?

____

____

____

____

3. Identify the scenes shown in the photos above. Where do they take place?

1. ______________________ **2.** ______________________

5 Choose a capital city and complete the table. Use the Internet to help you.

capital city	population	typical food	festival	climate

6 Read the texts and choose the correct answer.

1. This river runs through the towns of Cuenca, Albacete and Valencia. In 1982, this river broke through a dam and caused the biggest flood in Spanish history.

   a. Júcar   b. Tajo   c. Turia

2. This river is one of the most important rivers in the Iberian Peninsula. It is the second longest river in Spain. The source of the river is in Fontibre (Cantabria) and the mouth is in Tarragona.

   a. Jalón   b. Ebro   c. Segre

3. This river originates in Andalucía and flows south-west through Huelva. It has a reddish colour and has been mined for copper, gold, silver and other minerals.

   a. Tinto   b. Odiel   c. Guadiana

4. The name of this mountain range can be translated as 'snowy range' in English. It is in the south of the country in the region of Andalucía. It is a popular tourist destination especially because of its ski resorts.

   a. Sierra de Gredos   b. Sierra de Gata   c. Sierra Nevada

5. This mountain range is about 20km from the north coast of Spain. Some of the areas are popular with climbers, mountaineers and mountain walkers. The mountain range is located in Asturias, Cantabria and Castilla-León.

   a. Picos de Europa   b. Submeseta Norte   c. Montes de Toledo

7 Label the mountains on the map.

a. ____________________

b. ____________________

c. ____________________

d. ____________________

e. ____________________

f. ____________________

g. ____________________

h. ____________________

i. ____________________

8. Decide whether these rivers flow into the Cantabrian (C), the Atlantic (A) or the Mediterranean (M) watershed.

Tambre	☐	Llobregat	☐	Almanzora	☐
Navia	☐	Eo	☐	Vinalopo	☐
Ter	☐	Miño	☐	Guadalete	☐
Tajo	☐	Odiel	☐	Turia	☐

9. Read the definitions and write the correct words.

1. the place where a river flows into the sea:

   e____________________

2. groups of small islands:

   a____________________

3. a river that flows into a larger river:

   t____________________

4. the shape of the coast:

   c____________________

5. the place where a river begins:

   s____________________

10. Read the statements below. Who is in charge of decisions related to each one? Decide whether it is the Autonomous Community (AC) or the National Government (NG).

1. change the design of the flag ☐
2. change how taxes are collected ☐
3. think about town planning ☐
4. improve conditions for workers ☐
5. decide the official language ☐

Project work

11 You're going to prepare a quiz about an Autonomous Community or City. Use the categories from this list or your own ideas.

regional dishes · cities · tourist attractions · flags · languages · festivals · climate

12 Do some research to help you write 10 questions about the place of your choice. Write the questions in the table and the answers in your notebook. Then, ask two classmates the questions in your quiz.

questions	classmate 1	classmate 2

13 Once you've got all the answers, look at the quiz again and think about it.

1. Did you get all the answers correct? __________
2. Which questions were difficult? __________
3. How would you make the difficult questions easier? __________
4. How would you make the easy questions harder? __________
5. Give your revised quiz to two other classmates. Do they get better or worse results? __________

Skills check

14 Complete the text using the words from the box. You need to change the adjectives into the superlative form.

high	world	44	for
late	buildings	in	large

Spain has the third ______ number of World Heritage Sites in the world. Only China and Italy have more. Of Spain's ______ sites, 39 are cultural, 3 are natural and 2 are mixed.

Some of the ______ additions to the list were the mercury mines ______ Almadén, Castilla-La Mancha. Mercury trade between Europe and America has been important ______ centuries, so UNESCO believes it is in the interest of the international community to preserve this area.

The mines, and the surrounding ______, such as Retamar Castle, share their UNESCO status with Idrija in Slovenia. Together, they represent the two ______ mercury mines in the ______.

15 Complete the fact file about the Royal Site of San Lorenzo de El Escorial in Madrid. Use the words from the box.

21	1984	two	three	26	Felipe II

Fact file:

1. The King ______ commissioned the monastery in the 16th century.
2. ______ architects were in charge of construction: Juan Bautista de Toledo and Juan de Herrera.
3. It took ______ years to complete, from 1563-1584.
4. This place had ______ functions: as a Royal residence, a monastery and a burial crypt.
5. More than ______ people are buried in the crypt.
6. In ______ the UNESCO declared this place a World Heritage Site.

UNIT 3 Geography of Europe

1 Correct these statements about Europe.

1. Europe is the smallest continent.

2. There are 45 countries in Europe.

3. Russia is not in Europe but belongs to the European Union.

4. The biggest country in Europe by geographical area is Germany.

5. The Black Sea separates Europe from Africa.

6. About 75 per cent of the European population lives in rural areas.

7. Polar climate is found in the south of Europe.

2 Read about three European countries. Match the descriptions to the countries. Which climate do they have?

1. This country is transcontinental because part of it is in Asia and another part is in Europe. The flag is red with a white star and a crescent. This country does not belong to the European Union and does not use the euro. ☐ ______
2. This country is in central Europe and although it belongs to the European Union, it does not use the euro. Its current currency is the zloty. ☐ ______
3. This is a landlocked country in central Europe bordered by seven countries. The terrain is very mountainous. It belongs to the European Union and uses the euro. ☐ ______

a. Austria
b. Poland
c. Turkey

3 Look at the map and label it. Write the names of the countries and their capital cities.

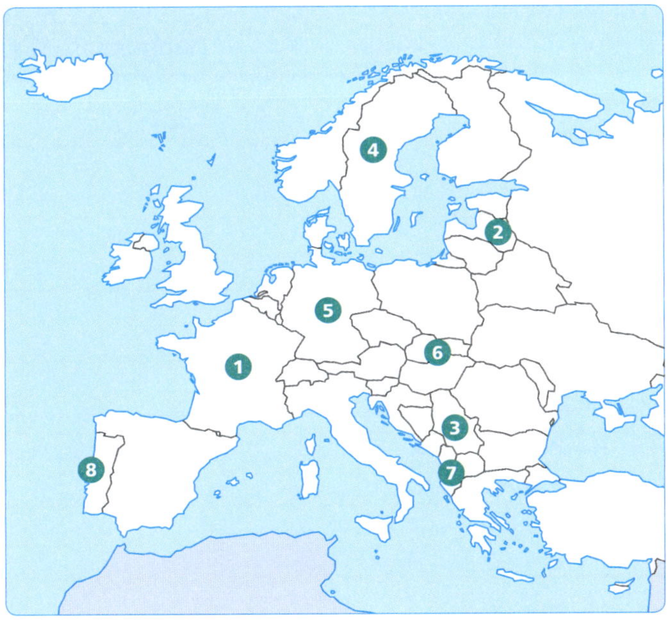

1. *France; Paris*
2. ______________________
3. ______________________
4. ______________________
5. ______________________
6. ______________________
7. ______________________
8. ______________________

4 Colour the map above to show the different climates in Europe.

5 Look at the map and answer the questions.

1. What countries does the strait of Gibraltar separate? ______________________

2. What is the name of the strait that separates the Black Sea and the Sea of Marmara? ______________________

3. Name three islands in the Mediterranean Sea. ______________________

4. Which country has borders with Spain and France? ______________________

5. Which bodies of water surround Greece? ______________________

6. Which countries border the Czech Republic? ______________________

6 Think about any differences between southern and northern Europe. Consider the following aspects and write a short text.

landforms	climate	education	leisure	languages

7 Choose the correct options to label the map correctly.

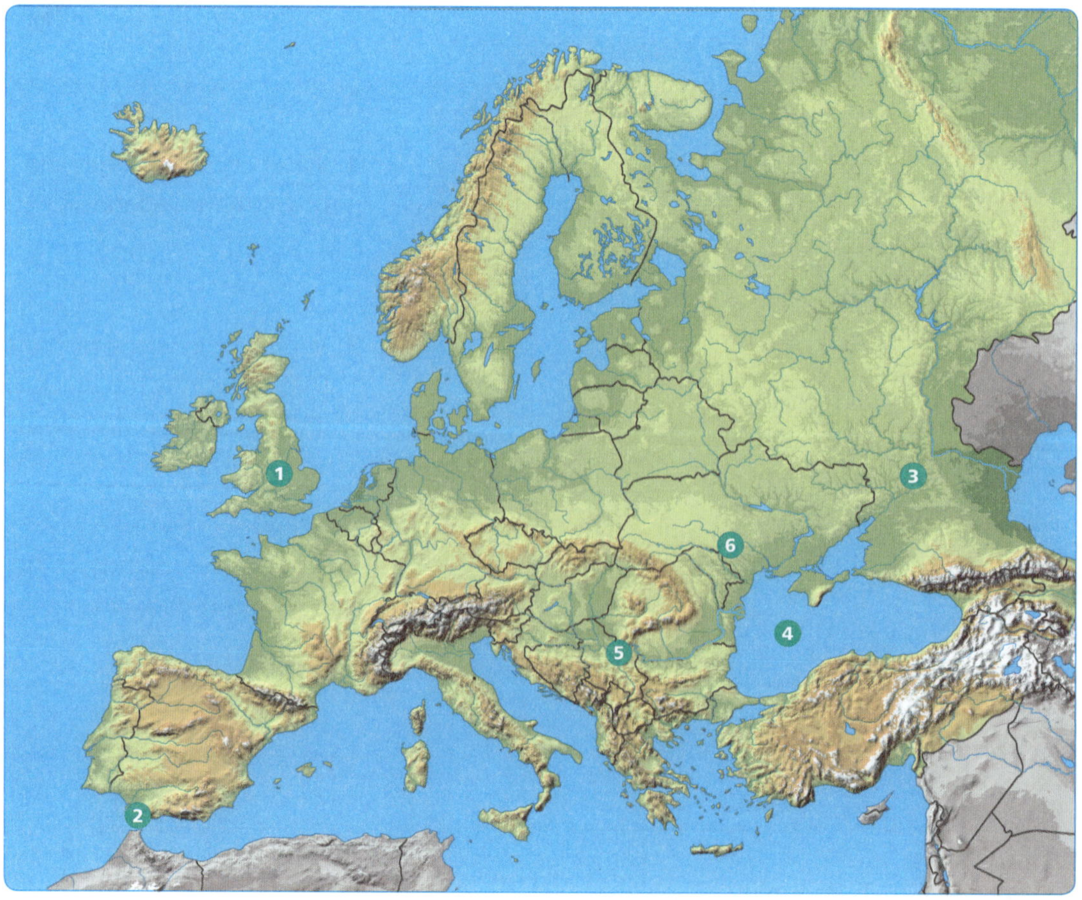

1. Appenines / Pennines
2. Str. of Gibraltar / Str. of Marmara
3. Don / Danube
4. Caspian Sea / Black Sea
5. Dinaric Alps / Transylvanian Alps
6. Dnieper / Dniester

8. Label the seas on the map.

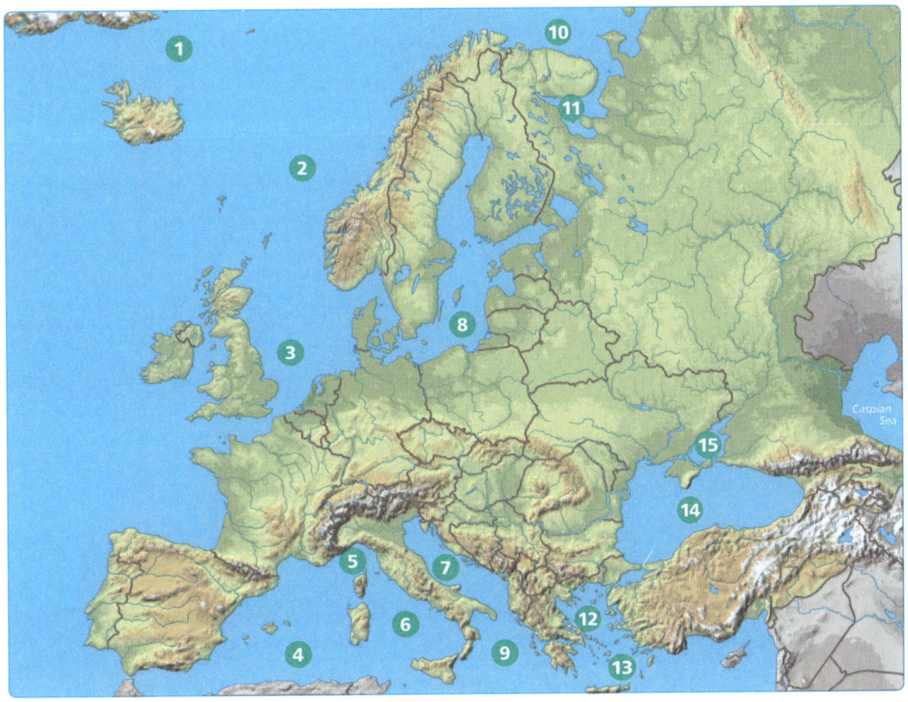

1. ______________________
2. ______________________
3. ______________________
4. ______________________
5. ______________________
6. ______________________
7. ______________________
8. ______________________
9. ______________________
10. ______________________
11. ______________________
12. ______________________
13. ______________________
14. ______________________
15. ______________________

9. Read the sentences about rivers and seas in Europe. Are the sentences true (T) or false (F)?

1. The Danube starts in Germany and flows across central Europe. ☐
2. The Danube is the longest river in Europe. ☐
3. The Thames flows into the North Sea. ☐
4. Sweden and Poland both have the Baltic Sea as their coastal waters. ☐

10. Read the definitions and write the correct words.

1. It means a country expands into two continents: t______________ c______________
2. The limit between two countries: b______________

Project work

11 Think about a European country and write a full sentence that is true for each of the following categories. Then, ask your classmates to read over the sentences and guess the name of the country.

1. political ruler: ____________________
2. population density: ____________________
3. economy: ____________________
4. wildlife: ____________________
5. rivers and mountains: ____________________
6. climate: ____________________
7. nationality: ____________________

12 How many categories did your classmates need to answer to guess the country?

____

13 Do Activity 10 again with another country.

14 Read the texts about Italy. Which of the above categories 1-7 is each text referring to? Write the correct number in the boxes.

1. Italy is an important route for certain bird species as it functions as a natural bridge on the flight path from one continent to another. In 2011, it was recorded that the country is home to more than 527 species, including 15 that are globally in danger. ☐
2. According to the law, Italian citizenship is automatically acquired if you are born to an Italian parent. You can also be granted it in special cases. For example, if you are resident in Italy and were born there to foreign parents. ☐
3. Italy is home to the western Alps which have rugged, high peaks. The Italian Alps are divided into three main groups depending where exactly in Italy they run through. Down the backbone of the country lie the Apennines, running down the full length of the peninsula. ☐

Skills check

15 Read this guide to Europe. Then answer the questions below.

In London you can take a ride on the London Eye which gives a spectacular view of London. You should also hire a bike and **observe** the Shard at night – the UK's tallest building. Then **hop over** to Paris to see the Eiffel Tower, built originally as a temporary exhibition. In Athens, the oldest modern Olympic stadium is a sight to **behold**. Visiting the Alps in Italy is also a great experience. There is **a wealth of** activities to enjoy. In winter, you can ski and in summer you can walk, cycle or do some mountaineering. You should remember that the climate is different depending on where you are on the continent. In some regions you'll enjoy a Mediterranean climate but mostly it will be a bit cold!

What do the bold words from the text mean? Circle the correct answers.

1. observe
   look at / hear / smell / love
2. hop over
   ride / cycle / swim / go quickly
3. behold
   look for / look at / be impressed by / run away
4. a wealth of
   a couple / many / a few / some

16 Correct the grammar mistakes in these sentences about islands in Europe.

1. An island is a piece of land surrounded of water.

   ____

2. Iceland and Ireland is an Island.

   ____

3. Great Britain is an island on the North Atlantic.

   ____

4. Sicily is the most big island in Italy.

   ____

UNIT 4 The European Union

1 Are the following statements about the EU true (T) or false (F)?

a. All European countries belong to the EU. ☐

b. The UK was one of the founding members of the EU. ☐

c. EU stands for 'European Union'. ☐

d. The EU was founded before World War II. ☐

e. All euro banknotes are the same colour. ☐

2 Read the text about the euro and answer the questions below.

In February 1992, the Maastricht Treaty was signed. This treaty established a timeline and the criteria for joining the eurozone. In May 1998, the euro was formally launched and was first introduced in its non-cash form in January 1999. Since then it has been called one of the most important economic events of all time. It wasn't until 2002 that participating countries could use actual euro coins and notes. Countries that belong to the EU and use the euro form the Eurozone. These countries had to give up their own currency so that a single monetary system could be created.

1. Which word (or words) from the text means 'officially'? ______
2. When was the euro introduced in its cash form? ______
3. What is the collective name given to countries that are using the euro? ______
4. Can participating countries use both their own currency and the euro? ______

3 Tick the countries that belong to the European Union.

a. Denmark ☐
b. Ireland ☐
c. Albania ☐
d. Finland ☐
e. Greece ☐
f. Netherlands ☐
g. Moldova ☐
h. Poland ☐
i. Norway ☐

4 Write the names of the countries from Activity 3 that do not use the euro.

______

______

5 Read the sentences about the euro coins and decide whether they are true or false. Then, rewrite the incorrect sentences correctly.

	true	false
1. There are seven different euro coins.	☐	☐
2. All the coins are the same on both sides.	☐	☐
3. One euro is divided into one hundred cents.	☐	☐
4. The coins symbolise the unity of the EU.	☐	☐
5. Not all the European Union member states use the euro.	☐	☐

____

____

6 Write about the benefits for a country of being a member of the EU. Use the following headings to help you.

- work: ____
- human rights: ____
- travel: ____
- goods and services: ____

7 Read the sentences and choose the correct institution they refer to.

1. This institution spends EU money.
   a. European Council   b. European Commission
2. Members of this institution discuss the political direction of the EU.
   a. European Council   b. Council of the EU
3. This institution shares budgeting decisions with the council of the EU.
   a. European Parliament   b. European Court of Auditors
4. This institution is the highest court in the EU.
   a. European Court of Auditors   b. Court of Justice of the EU

8 Look at the photos of famous things from countries in the European Union. Label them with the names in the box.

a

b

c

d

e

Austria
Finland
England
Greece
France

9 Read about four different EU policies and match them to the correct category below.

1 This policy is dedicated to putting a 'cap and trade' on certain greenhouse gases. It is all about limiting the harmful substances some industries produce.

2 This policy is dedicated to promoting research integrity. It is all about adopting guidelines and codes of conduct.

3 This policy is dedicated to 'the right to be forgotten'. It is all about online search engines protecting a person's data.

4 This policy is dedicated to removing existing barriers of trade, allowing freedom of movement. It is all about creating a user-friendly environment.

citizen's rights	climate action	science and technology	business

10 Complete these sentences about the single market in Europe.

a. A single market is ______

b. It exists because ______

c. People are free to ______

d. Workers ______

e. The cost ______

11 Answer the questions about languages in the EU.

a. Is there one official language in the EU?

____

b. Do you think all European citizens should speak the same language? Write one advantage and one disadvantage.

____

____

c. How many languages can you speak?

____

12 Read about the process of joining the European Union. Fill in the gaps with the words from the box.

approved	democratic	Turkey	negotiations
applicant	stable	human rights	administrative

When a new country wants to join the EU, it has to apply to the European Council. The Council bases its decision on the advice of two other institutions: the Commission and the Parliament. The _______________ country must be _______________ and protect _______________. It also has to be economically _______________. It must be ready to adapt its _______________ systems to fit in with the way the EU works. If the application is accepted, the next stage involves a series of _______________ with the other EU member states. _______________ wants to be in the EU and its application was _______________ in 1999. Negotiations started in 2005 and have still not finished.

13 List the European countries that are not EU member states.

____

____

____

Project work

14 What new EU policies would you like to introduce? Explain your new policies and why they would be a good idea.

1. culture

2. employment

3. social rights

15 Compare your ideas with your classmates'. Are your ideas similar? Did anybody else in the class think of the same ideas?

16 Record the information in your notebook and vote for the most interesting ones.

17 Design a slogan for each policy in Activity 14.

1

2

3

Skills check

18 Read the text and circle the correct words.

The European employment strategy *seeks / decides* to create more and better jobs. It aims to do this by targeting different areas:

1. Youth on the move: its aim is to *improve / make easier* the quality of training and education received in different countries.
2. New and appropriate skills: its aim is to encourage and support people to get the right skills for particular *studies / jobs*.
3. Reducing poverty: its aim is to direct training and education *towards / from* all kinds of people at all levels of society.

19 Write sentences using the words you have chosen in Activity 18.

a. ______________________________

____

b. ______________________________

____

c. ______________________________

____

d. ______________________________

____

20 Answer the questions related to the text in Activity 18.

a. Do you think it is a good policy?

____

b. Why or why not?

____

c. What is difficult about implementing this kind of policy?

____

UNIT 5 The economy

1 Match each economic sector to the correct definition.

a. Primary sector	**1.** This is the sector which provides services to customers.
b. Secondary sector	**2.** This sector obtains products directly from nature.
c. Tertiary sector	**3.** This sector manufactures new products from raw materials.

2 Which activity do these photos show? Choose the correct word from the box and indicate the economic sector they belong to.

tourism	farming	food industry	fishing	healthcare	construction

a

Activity: *healthcare*

Sector: *tertiary sector*

b

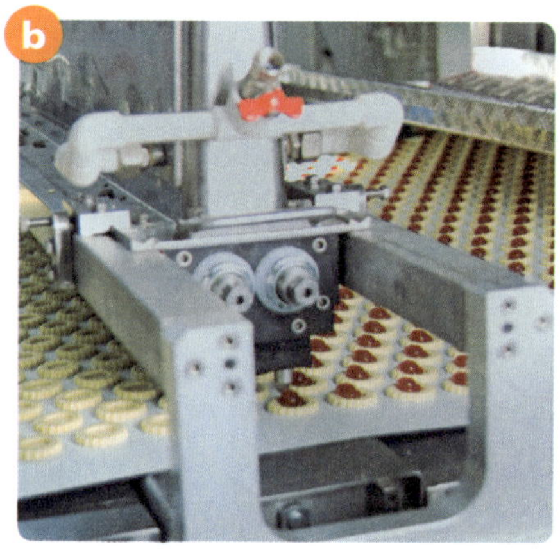

Activity: ____________

Sector: ____________

c

Activity: ____________

Sector: ____________

d

Activity: ____________

Sector: ____________

e

Activity: ____________

Sector: ____________

f

Activity: ____________

Sector: ____________

3 Complete these diagrams about raw materials and manufactured products.

food industry

raw materials		manufactured products
peaches		*peach marmalade*
______		______
______		______

textile industry

raw materials		manufactured products
cotton		*cotton T-shirts*
______		______
______		______

4 Read the text and choose the best word for each space.

Today 5 per cent of the (1) ______ population of Spain works in the primary sector. This is 55 per cent less than at the beginning of the 20th century.

Olives and (2) ______ are the main crops in Spain, although potatoes, cereals, and vegetables are also grown. In the field of livestock farming, pig farming is an important activity, mainly in (3) ______.

Since Spain has many kilometres of coast, (4) ______ is an important activity, too. Mining is not as important as it was in the past, but there is still some notable mining activity in Asturias.

Spain's secondary sector is (5) ______ in size. About 30 per cent of the active population works in this sector. There are important (6) ______ in Bilbao, Barcelona and Madrid.

1. active / passive / rural
2. rice / oranges / apples
3. Galicia / Aragón / Extremadura
4. tourism / farming / fishing
5. growing / decreasing / falling
6. industries / products / materials

5 **Complete the definitions with the correct words from the box.**

construction	capital	energy	base	consumer

a. ____________ industries transform raw materials into semi-finished products.

b. ____________ industries use raw materials to make buildings and public works.

c. ____________ goods industries use base industry products to make machinery and equipment.

d. ____________ goods industries use products produced by the base and capital goods industries to make new products and sell them to customers.

6 **Complete the diagram using the words in the box and describe the process. Some words can be used more than once.**

~~primary sector~~	secondary sector	tertiary sector
domestic trade	textile industry	consumer goods industry

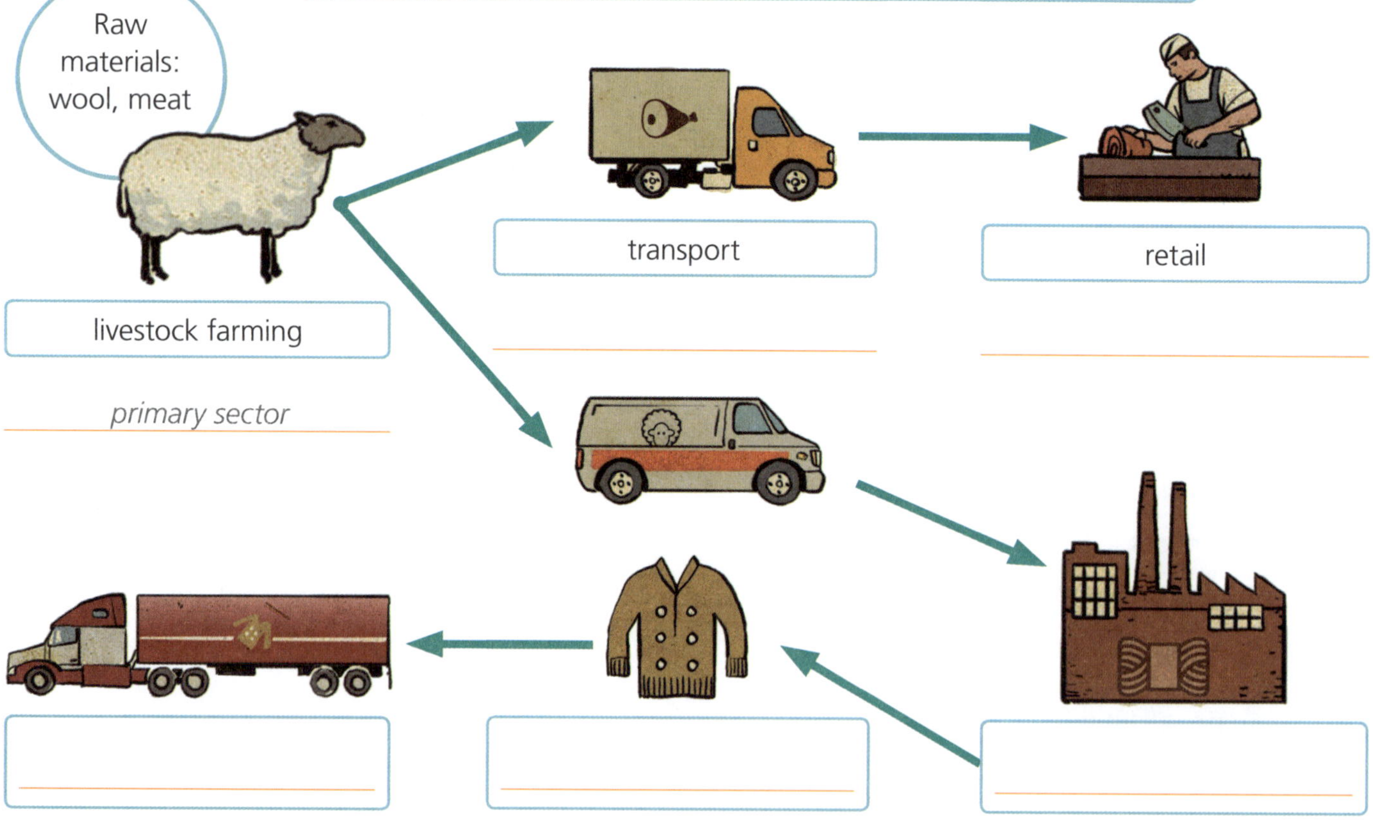

____

____

7 Complete and colour the diagram according to the facts.

Economic sectors in Europe	
Economic sector	**% of active population**
Primary sector	4 %
Secondary sector	30 %
Tertiary sector	66 %

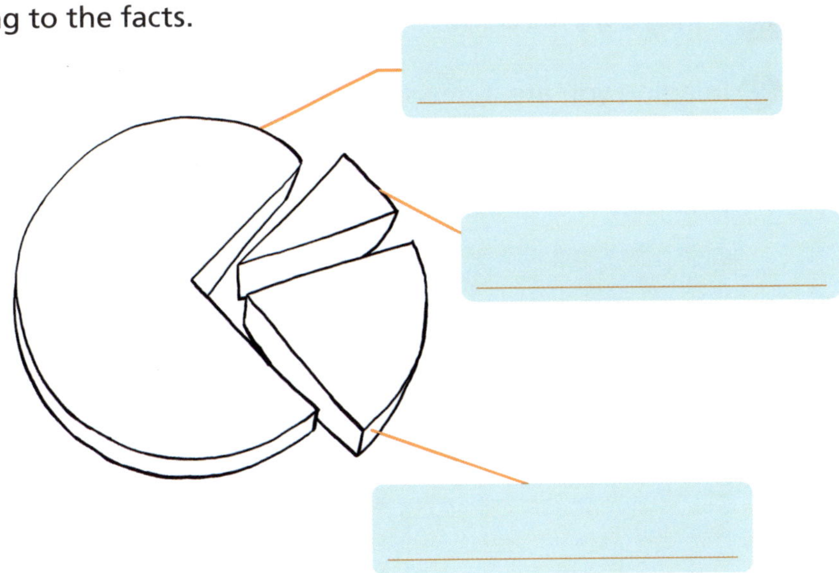

8 Find the names of 15 jobs and classify them in the correct economic sector.

T	C	A	R	P	E	N	T	E	R	A	W	X	F
T	F	T	N	U	H	B	W	E	T	C	M	C	A
U	R	E	K	B	L	B	U	I	L	D	E	R	C
Y	C	A	G	L	E	P	K	N	P	A	B	A	T
B	P	C	N	I	M	H	E	L	O	H	F	F	O
E	V	H	D	S	A	A	C	M	V	T	I	T	R
E	H	E	O	H	L	F	B	X	M	H	S	S	Y
K	E	R	N	E	N	A	O	V	I	P	H	M	W
E	N	X	W	R	K	R	T	Q	N	N	E	A	O
E	L	U	D	E	D	M	A	O	E	D	R	N	R
P	A	B	R	D	T	E	D	P	R	A	M	E	K
E	O	M	X	S	W	R	D	V	A	W	A	C	E
R	G	A	R	D	E	N	E	R	U	V	N	U	R
G	R	S	H	E	P	H	E	R	D	E	L	P	C

primary sector jobs	*farmer,*
secondary sector jobs	
tertiary sector jobs	

Project work

9 Imagine you are a newspaper journalist who is interested in Spanish traditional crafts. Do some research to find out what raw materials and tools are needed for these crafts and which products are made.

Guitar making	
Materials	
Tools	
Products	

Damascening	
Materials	
Tools	
Products	

Lace making	
Materials	
Tools	
Products	

Marquetry	
Materials	
Tools	
Products	

10 Choose the craft you like most and write a short text about it. Tell your readers about its origin and their importance today.

Skills check

11 Read the text about honey bee industry crafts and circle the correct words.

Honeybees have an organized society. Some bees have specific roles in the *colony / members:* guards, nurses, construction workers etc. The queen can live for several years while worker bees live for 6 weeks during summer and 4-9 months during winter. Bees are very *busy / inactive* during summer months but they are quite inactive during the winter.

Bees are essential to *agriculture / forestry*. Most of our crops depend greatly on the honeybee for *pollination / fertilization*. Without them there would be a significant *decrease / increase* in fruits and vegetables. Unfortunately, these insects are in danger of dissappearing due to some farming practices and diseases. The care provided by beekeepers is the reason why most bee colonies are alive.

Beekeeping and honey collection date back to the Stone Age. The *harvest / crop* of the bee products provide us with honey, pollen, royal jelly, wax and propolis, which can be eaten or used in craft, manufacturing and medicine. Honeybee products are of high nutritional value and have many applications.

12 Write sentences using the words you have chosen in Activity 11.

a. ______________________________

b. ______________________________

c. ______________________________

d. ______________________________

e. ______________________________

f. ______________________________

13 Complete this mind map with the information from the text in Activity 11.

Honeybees			
How do they live?	Why are they so important?	Who takes care of them?	Products and benefits
______	______	______	______
______	______	______	______

Business and money

1 Complete the text about money using the words from the box.

exchanging	bartering	trade	money
bank	currency	value	coins

Money is an important invention of civilization. It is essential to the development of _____________. People have been using money for more than 3000 years. Before using _____________, people used a system called _____________________________, which consists of _____________________________ goods and services between two people.

Bartering is a slow system of exchange, since people have to discuss and agree on the _____________ of the goods or services they exchange.

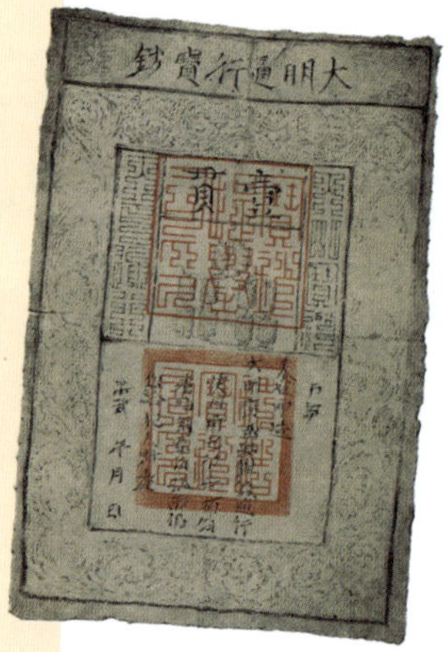

The need for making trade easier led to the use of _____________. First, people used valuable objects or small replicas of the objects they exchanged instead of the objects themselves. These evolved into the first _____________ made of gold, silver or other metals.

Around 600 BC the Chinese invented paper money which could be exchanged for gold or silver coins at a _____________.

2 Make a list of goods or services you could offer and fix a value for them. What do you think you could get for them?

bartering	
goods I could offer	goods I would like to get

③ Where is this currency used? Match the banknotes to their symbol and country(ies).

1

yuan

2

pound sterling

3

euro

4

American dollar

5

rouble

6

yen

	Symbol	Country
	€	China
	₽	Europe
	¥	Russia
	$	UK
1	¥	Japan
	£	USA

④ Complete the sentences using the words from the box.

loan	entrepreneur	insurance	salary	office	loss

a. Startup costs are the expenses an ____________ has before opening a business.

b. A ____________ is the money someone gets from a bank which must be returned in a fixed period of time.

c. Rent is the money to be paid in order to be able to use a building, such as an ____________ or a store.

d. Insurance is a contract between an ____________ company and a client. The client pays in order to protect their business from any kind of ____________, accident or damage.

e. Staff are the people an entrepreneur contracts to work for him/her for a ____________.

5 Complete the sentences about variable costs.

a. An ad campaign is part of the ________________ costs.

b. Delivering products to the costumers produces ________________ costs.

c. Materials used to make a product or package it are part of the ________________ costs.

d. Employees who meet their sales targets receive ________________.

e. Employees get ________________ for the sales they make.

6 Imagine you are to start a small business. Think about your ongoing and variable costs. Complete the table.

	"Bikes and Wings. Messengers"	"Homemade Deli-cakes"
Will you ask for a loan?		
Will you rent a place?		
Will you take out insurance?		
Will you employ someone? What job would he / she do?		
What materials do you need to make your products?		
How would you advertise your business?		

7 Read the examples and add five more ways of using money under each heading.

How can I earn money?

Selling things on a street market ______________________

______________________ ______________________

______________________ ______________________

How can I save money?

Buying fewer sweets ______________________

______________________ ______________________

______________________ ______________________

How can I spend my money?

Making a donation to an NGO ______________________

______________________ ______________________

______________________ ______________________

8 Read and decide if these transactions count as income (**I**), fixed expenses (**FE**) or variable expenses (**VE**).

a. You receive your pocket money: 20 € [ ]

b. You buy your favourite perfume: 17 € [ ]

c. You sell old videogames to a friend: 12 € [ ]

d. You do the shopping for your grandad and he gives you some cash: 2,70 € [ ]

e. You invite your best friend to the cinema: 13 € [ ]

f. A neighbour asks you to take care of her little child: 15 € [ ]

g. You buy your weekly comic: 6,50 € [ ]

Project work

9 What currency is used in other parts of the world? Do some research to complete this table.

Europe	Australasia
Switzerland: ______	India: ______
Netherlands: ______	Kuwait: ______
Denmark: ______	South Korea: ______
Finland: ______	Australia: ______
North and South America	**Africa**
Mexico: ______	Morocco: ______
Cuba: ______	South Africa: ______
Chile: ______	Mali: ______
Canada: ______	Egypt: ______

10 What is a bitcoin? Look it up on the Internet and answer the questions.

a. Who created the bitcoin?

______

b. When was it created?

______

c. What is its symbol?

______

Skills check

11 Read this text about microfinance and circle the correct words.

Microfinance is a banking system in which financial institutions offer financial services to the *poor / rich*, such as loans, insurance or savings accounts, to help them climb out of *poverty / illness*. The idea of microfinance was started in Bangladesh by the economist and banker Muhammad Yunus, who founded the first *bank / insurance company* for the poor, the Grameen Bank.

Microfinance involves *lending / borrowing* small amounts of money which people use to start a small business. Thanks to these microcredits many people have become *micro-entrepreneurs / employees*, have taken care of their families and improved their lives.

Today there are thousands of microfinance institutions; many of them develop training courses for the *borrowers / lenders* in which they learn how to save and how to *spend / waste* their money.

90 per cent of the borrowers all over the world are women. When a woman improves her life, the first ones to benefit are her *children / neighbours*. They get new opportunities and are able to access *education / entertainment* and health care. Through microcredits new businesses emerge which *deny / provide* new valuable goods and services to the community.

Anyone can become a moneylender. There are many NGOs which offer people the opportunity to lend their money to people who need it.

12 Read the text in Activity 11 again and answer the questions.

a. Why is it called microfinance?

____

b. Where did this idea come from?

____

c. Who founded the first bank for the poor?

____

d. Who benefits from microcredits?

____

e. How do their communities benefit from microcredits?

____

UNIT 7 Modern Spain I

1 Read the text about absolutism and answer the questions below.

The term absolutism refers to a **sole** person holding all of the power. It could relate to many different areas such as politics, truth and the monarchy. This is not an **exhaustive** list. In politics the term means that one party has power over everyone. Absolutism in terms of the truth refers to a thought being absolutely true or absolutely false. An absolute monarchy means that a certain government has the power to freely rule their land with no **opposition**.

What do the bold words from the text mean? Circle the correct answers.

1. sole

   a. single b. special c. powerful d. destructive

2. exhaustive

   a. big b. small c. dominating d. complete

3. opposition

   a. opponent b. supporter c. monarch d. problem

4. Write your own opinion about absolutism.

   ____

   ____

2 Make a list of some advantages and disadvantages of absolutism in the given categories.

	absolute truth	absolute politics	absolute monarchy
advantages			
disadvantages			

3 Cross the odd one out.

a. Industrial Revolution / 1789 / Spinning Jenny / factory

b. Carlos IV / absolutism / mutiny / abdication

c. merchant / lawyer / banker / doctor

d. Venezuela / Colombia / Bolivia / Paraguay

4. Match the principles of the Spanish Constitution of 1812 with their definitions.

1. free trade
2. male suffrage
3. freedom of the press

a. Expression and communication through different mediums were introduced.
b. All men were made equal and were given the right to vote.
c. A competitive market without barriers was introduced.

5. Complete the sentences about King Fernando VII.

a. Fernando was C________________ 's son.

b. His reign is divided into t________________ periods.

c. During the first years of his reign, a ________________ was the form of Government in Spain.

d. The heir to the throne was supposed to be his b________________ Carlos.

e. Fernando VII chose his daughter I________________ to be his successor after his death.

6. Read about the Ominous Decade. Then, describe the meanings of the terms in bold.

The Ominous Decade refers to the last ten years that King Fernando VII ruled Spain. This period saw the re-establishment of **strict censorship**, the formation of **royalist volunteers** who were against the Liberals and the introduction of a **decree** that allowed women to become heirs to the throne.

1. **strict censorship**

____

2. **royalist volunteers**

____

3. **decree**

____

7. Identify the social classes in 19th century Spain. Write U for upper class, M for middle class or W for working class.

a. doctor ☐
b. agricultural worker ☐
c. lawyer ☐
d. factory owner ☐
e. banker ☐
f. factory worker ☐

8. Make a list of some differences between the upper class and the working class.

9. Read the following sentences. What do they mean?

1. The upper class raised their social status by marrying into nobility.

2. The working class had few opportunities to improve their social status.

3. Industrial workers worked in dangerous conditions.

4. Workers demanded improvements in their wages.

10 Look at these paintings by Francisco de Goya. Write a short description of each one. Think about the ideas in the box.

disposition	colours	facial expressions	time reflected

1. ____________________

2. ____________________

11 Use the Internet to search for a painting by Goya that you like. Answer the questions.

a. What is it supposed to represent? What's the main theme?

b. What emotions does it provoke?

c. Why do you like it?

Project work

12 Imagine you live in Spain in 1812. You have been asked to propose some new principles for the Constitution. Add your ideas to the categories below.

obligations	prohibitions

13 Look at the list of obligations you have written in Activity 12 and add a list of advantages for each one.

Listing advantages

- The advantages are ...
- The benefits are ...
- The strengths are ...

Skills check

14 Read about absolutism in Spain. Choose the best word for each space.

As a result (1) ______ absolutism in 19th century, Spanish forces, under Fernando VII, started arriving in the American colonies. This began (2) ______ 1814 and was quite successful. Spain managed (3) ______ control the majority of these colonies. However, after just a couple (4) ______ years, Spanish rule ended (5) ______ Colombia. Many other colonies followed suit shortly after. By 1820, most of the empire was lost and King Fernando VII wasn't happy (6) ______ the result and decided to regain control. This created many problems.

1. in / on / of / to
2. on / in / around / with
3. to / of / in / from
4. with / from / of / to
5. of / on / from / in
6. in / of / on / with

15 Give your opinion on the Salic Law.

Useful language

- In my opinion, ...
- I think / I believe ...
- From my point of view, ...

UNIT 8 Modern Spain II

① **Read the statements about Spanish colonies. Are the sentences true (T) or false (F)?**

1. Spain lost Cuba in 1899. ☐

2. Spain lost Puerto Rico in 1898. ☐

3. Argentina was the first Spanish colony to become independent. ☐

4. The USA occupied Cuba, the Philippines and Puerto Rico in 1898. ☐

5. The Spanish converted all the inhabitants of their colonies to Catholicism. ☐

② **Read these texts about three Spanish colonies. Can you identify the country the texts refer to? Look at the flags to help you find the answers.**

1. ____________________

This country became a Spanish colony after the arrival of Columbus. The capital was briefly occupied by Great Britain. It was then exchanged for Florida and returned to Spain.

2. ____________________

The Spanish conquered this territory in 1521. It was officially declared independent in 1821.

3. ____________________

In 1532, the emperor from this country, Atahualpa, was captured and executed under Francisco Pizarro's rule. The Spanish colonisation of this country involved a long war. It took several years to occupy, but was eventually conquered in 1542. It officially gained its independence in 1821.

3 Look at the photos of famous things from Spanish colonies. Label them with the names from the box.

Mexico	Morocco	Panama	Argentina	Peru	Cuba

a

b

c

d

e

f

4 Look at the map and tick the correct sentences.

a. This map shows the territories Spain conquered in the 19th and 20th centuries. ☐

b. This map shows when Spain lost her colonies. ☐

c. Chile was the last Spanish colony in America to become independent. ☐

d. All the Spanish colonies were in America. ☐

e. Spain only had one colony on the African continent. ☐

5. Read the text about the differences between an absolute monarch and a constitutional monarch.

An absolute monarch holds all the power **whereas** a constitutional monarch has limited power. **This means that** an absolute monarch is not controlled by a constitution or the law. The king or queen of a constitutional monarchy rules **alongside** parliament. The system of constitutional monarchy was introduced to **prevent** kings and queens from abusing their powers. Another name for an absolute monarchy is an 'undemocratic' monarchy **while** another name for a constitutional monarchy is a 'liberal' monarchy.

What do the words in bold mean? Circle the correct answers.

1. whereas
   a. but b. similar to
2. this means that
   a. it's different b. it signifies
3. alongside
   a. allowing b. with
4. prevent
   a. interrupt b. stop
5. while
   a. whereas b. equally

6. "A good absolute monarch can be very advantageous but a bad monarch with absolute powers can be extremely dangerous." Do you agree with this sentence? Why / Why not? Justify your answer.

7. Answer the questions.

a. Can you name any absolute monarchs?

b. Which Constitution allowed women to vote?

c. Why do you think the Constitution of 1931 led to conflict with the Church?

d. Which Constitution is Spain governed by nowadays?

8 Read about the Restoration period in Spain. Fill in the gaps with the words from the box.

conservative	Constitution	liberal	Restoration

On 29 December 1874, after almost a century of political instability and civil wars, the ______________ period started. It lasted from Alfonso XII's reign through to Alfonso XIII's. Its aim was to turn things around in terms of politics and war. Spain soon became a constitutional monarchy, stated in the ______________ of 1876, and things began to change. During King Alfonso XII's reign, two key figures were Prime Ministers in the new political system: Antonio Cánovas del Castillo, from the ______________ party and Práxedes Mateo Sagasta, from the ______________ party. The economy improved and modernisation of the country took place on a grand scale.

9 Complete the timeline. Use the names from the box.

Alfonso XIII	Amadeo I de Saboya	Isabel II	Alfonso XII

1833-1868	1870-1873	1873-1874	1875-1885	1885-1902	1902-1931
______	______	*first republic*	______	*regency of María Cristina*	______

10 Think of some rules for both a democratic society and a dictatorial society in the given topics. What would a dictator and a democrat say about each of the ideas you have proposed?

topic	dictator	democrat
gender and equality		
voting		
trade		
press and communication		

Project work

11 Look at the photos. In what ways are they connected to Spain?

a

b

c

12 Write about the influence that Spanish culture has had on other countries or cultures. Can you think of any ways Spain and Spanish culture has had an influence on other countries? List your answers below.

influence	consequence
the Spanish language	*more than 20 sovereign states currently use it as an official language*

13 Can you identify the Spanish festivals shown in the photos and where they take place? Write a short description of each one.

a

b

Skills check

14 Write definitions for the words.

a. assassinate *(verb)*: ______

b. exile *(noun)*: ______

c. support *(verb)*: ______

d. bankruptcy *(noun)*: ______

e. ban *(verb)*: ______

15 Read about life under the Francoist regime and choose the best preposition for each space.

a. General Franco admitted, at one point, that more than 20 000 people were sent (1) ______ prison for their political beliefs.

b. Spanish was the only official language (2) ______ Spain.

c. Although other languages were forbidden, people spoke their languages (3) ______ private.

d. A vast secret police network was created to spy (4) ______ people.

e. Women were prevented (5) ______ doing certain jobs.

f. Freedom (6) ______ the press was restricted.

1. in / for / to
2. from / of / in
3. in / on / at
4. over / above / on
5. of / from / by
6. in / with / of

16 Imagine you were living in a rural area during the Francoist era. Describe a typical day in your life.

______

______

______

______

______

Spain today

1. The dates in the sentences below are incorrect. Rewrite the sentences correctly.

a. Spain became a democracy in 1976.

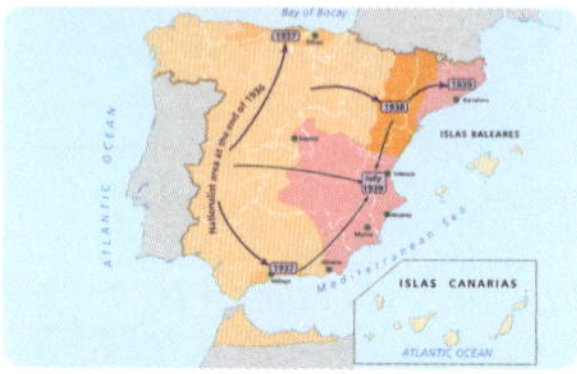

b. The Spanish Civil War started in 1926 and ended in 1929.

c. General Francisco Franco won the war for the Nationalists in 1929.

d. Juan Carlos became King of Spain in 1972.

2. Read the text about the Spanish Constitution. Decide whether the sentences below are true (T) or false (F).

After the death of Franco, Spain's present-day Constitution of 1978 was drawn up by different political groups in Spain. Eventually, it was approved in December of the same year. The Constitution means that Spain is now a social and democratic state governed by law.

The present-day Constitution came into effect on 1 January 1979. As a result, Spanish regions could become autonomous. The first ones to do so were the País Vasco and Cataluña, soon followed by Galicia.

The Constitution also recognises that the official language of the state is Castilian. Every citizen should learn it, and everyone has the right to speak it.

a. The present-day Constitution was drawn up before Franco died. ☐

b. Spain is now a social and democratic state. ☐

c. The Constitution meant that some regions could become independent. ☐

d. The Constitution gave a degree of autonomy to some regions. ☐

e. Spanish citizens can only speak Castilian. ☐

3 Read the text about the British constitutional monarchy and choose the best word for each space.

The British monarchy has two main (1) *responsibilities*. The first one is (2) ________. This means the king or queen has certain tasks to peform that have been defined over one thousand years of history. These tasks include opening (3) ________ and having meetings with the (4) ________. The monarchy also has to represent Britain to the rest of the world and make visits (5) ________ to other countries.

The other main responsibility is 'Head of Nation'. This job means that the monarch must encourage national (6) ________ and pride. This is done by regular (7) ________ throughout the whole of the United Kingdom in order to meet people from all walks of life.

1. works / job / ~~responsibilities~~ / members
2. Head of State / Head of UK / State manager / Monarch
3. shops / Parliament / jobs / Government
4. public / president / famous people / Prime Minister
5. by boat / by plane / by car / overseas
6. identity / speech / fun / rules
7. visits / walks / journeys / work

4 Complete the table with more examples.

Autonomous Community	Province	Municipality
Castilla y León	*León*	*Astorga*

5 Read the questions related to the Spanish Constitution. Choose the correct answers.

1. What is a referendum?
   a. a document that outlines people's opinions
   b. a vote
2. What is 'national sovereignty'?
   a. a term that means that a group or person has supreme authority
   b. a type of governmental organisation
3. What does political pluralism allow?
   a. peaceful coexistence of differences
   b. the existence of one absolute idea
4. What does 'tolerance' refer to?
   a. the rejection of different opinions and beliefs
   b. the polite and peaceful acceptance of differences

6 Write about the rights and responsibilities that Spanish citizens have.

Rights

____

____

Responsibilities

____

____

7 Research different political parties in Spain and complete the information in the table.

political party	when was the party founded and by whom?	what is their political stance?	ideology

8 Match the functions to the correct Spanish ministries from the box.

the ministry of Foreign Affairs and Cooperation	the ministry of Public Works
the ministry of the Interior	the ministry of Education, Culture and Sport

1. ______

- *deal with Spain's external policies*
- *develop Spain's relationships with other nations*
- *promote and defend human rights*

2. ______

- *prepare and implement government policy related to land transport and infrastructure*
- *manage and direct postal services*

3. ______

- *improve road safety*
- *promote conditions for freedom and personal safety*
- *deal with immigration issues*

4. ______

- *improve the quality of education*
- *initiate and develop overseas programmes*
- *offer grants and scholarships*

9 Complete the diagram about the three powers that are established in the Spanish Constitution.

Three powers

- ______
  - lower chamber: ______ (deputies)
  - upper chamber: ______ (senators)
- executive
  - Government: ______ ______
- ______
  - judges and magistrates
    - judicial bodies: ______ ______

Project work

10 Imagine you are the the King or Queen of the United Kingdom. Brainstorm ideas about your role in the UK.

personal life	roles and responsibilities	reasons why you like being a Monarch	disadvantages of being a Monarch

11 Use the information from Activity 10 to write a letter to a dictator about your role.

Dear ______________________,

I'm writing to tell you about

____

____

____

____

____

12 Do you think the dictator has the same roles and responsibilities as a constitutional monarch? Justify your answer.

____

____

____

____

Skills check

13 Read the text and choose the best word for each space.

The Fathers of the Constitution were seven (1) ____________ leaders who worked together to write the Spanish Constitution in (2) ____________. Even though these leaders came from different political (3) ____________ and had very different political beliefs, they had the ability to (4) ____________, respect and understand each other. They also believed in the fundamental values of a democratic society. These values are justice, freedom, equality and a respect for differences. The Constitution was approved by (5) ____________ on 31 October 1978 and by the Spanish citizens in a (6) ____________ on 6 December 1978.

1. political / economic / artistic
2. 1987 / 1978 / 1998
3. houses / schools / parties
4. listen / fight / read
5. judges / Parliament / courts
6. referendum / manifesto / campaign

14 Choose the best word to represent your ideas. Compare with a friend.

a. You *shouldn't / can / can't* discriminate against people because of their religion.
b. You *shouldn't / mustn't / don't have to* vote in elections in Spain.
c. We *have to / don't have to* respect the law.
d. Education *is / isn't* a right.

15 Read the definitions and write the correct words.

a. This person chooses the ministers who will be in charge of the different ministries: ____________

b. This ministry is responsible for national security and immigration issues: ____________

c. This person makes sure the Autonomous Communities do not violate the Constitution.

d. It is the official language in Spain: ____________

Glossary

English	Your language	English	Your language

Unit 1: Planet Earth

English	Your language
anemometer (n)	
atmospheric pressure (n)	
axis (n)	
barometer (n)	
cardinal point (n)	
collect (v)	
cool (v)	
core (n)	
cosmic dust (n)	
crust (n)	
drop (n)	
drought (n)	
environment (n)	
exosphere (n)	
float (v)	
galaxy (n)	
glacier (n)	
harmful (adj)	
heat (v)	
humidity (n)	
hurricane (n)	
hygrometer (n)	
iceberg (n)	
layer (n)	
magnetic field (n)	
mantle (n)	
mesosphere (n)	
Moon (n)	
orbit (v)	
oxygen (n)	
ozone layer (n)	
planet (n)	
pumps (n)	
radiation (n)	
rain gauge (n)	
revolution (n)	
rotation (n)	
sand (n)	
season (n)	
solidify (v)	
stratosphere (n)	
stream (n)	
sunlight (n)	
thermometer (n)	
thermosphere (n)	
troposphere (n)	

UNIT 2: Geography of Spain

English	Your language
accommodation (n)	
beach (n)	
border (v)	
cape (n)	
cliff (n)	
coast (n)	
coastline (n)	
compulsory (adj)	
coral reef (n)	
councilor (n)	
course (n)	
crowd (n)	
dam (n)	
depression (n)	
detergent (n)	
estuary (n)	
fat (n)	
feed (v)	
flat (adj)	
harbour (n)	
island (n)	
lake (n)	
leak (v)	
mayor (n)	

English	Your language
mountain (n)	
mouth (n)	
oil tank (n)	
pesticide (n)	
pilgrim (n)	
plain (n)	
relief (n)	
researcher (n)	
reservoir (n)	
river (n)	
rocky (adj)	
sandy (adj)	
sea level (n)	
sewage system (n)	
sink (n)	
soap (n)	
stormy (adj)	
tomb (n)	
treatment plant (n)	
tributary (n)	
watershed (n)	
wildlife (n)	

Glossary

English	Your language	English	Your language

UNIT 3: Geography of Europe

English	Your language	English	Your language
bears (n)		irrigation (n)	
beauty (n)		landmark (n)	
bogland (n)		landmass (n)	
bridge (n)		lynx (n)	
cultural diversity (n)		medium-sized (adj)	
cut down (v)		ocean (n)	
dish (n)		outstanding (adj)	
environmental organisation (n)		peak (n)	
		peat bog (n)	
floods (n)		rains (n)	
forest (n)		road (n)	
frozen (adj)		sea (n)	
gas pipeline (n)		snails (n)	
		strait (n)	
groundwater (n)		strawberry (n)	
height (n)		threat (n)	
heritage (n)		wetland (n)	
hydroelectric (adj)		wolves (n)	

Unit 4: The European Union

English	Your language
abroad (adv)	
anthem (n)	
audit (n)	
banknote (n)	
barrier (n)	
coin (n)	
competition entry (n)	
consulate (n)	
consumption rate (n)	
counterfeit (adj)	
currency (n)	
customs (n)	
customs charges (n)	
death penalty (n)	
degree (n)	
disease (n)	
embassy (n)	
enterprise (n)	
exchange (n)	
foreign (adj)	
founding member (n)	
goods (n)	
grant (n)	
graph (n)	
growth (n)	
join (v)	
labelling (n)	
loan (n)	
member state (n)	
motto (n)	
peace-keeper (n)	
proposal (n)	
resource (n)	
reunite (v)	
single market (n)	
steel (n)	
strengthen (v)	
strong (adj)	
target (n)	
treaty (n)	
tuition fees (n)	
wasteful (adj)	
weight (n)	

Glossary

UNIT 5: The economy

English	Your language
active population (n)	
capital (n)	
consumer (n)	
crafts (n)	
domestic trade (n)	
energy industry (n)	
fishing (n)	
food industry (n)	
foreign trade (n)	
goods (n)	
harvest (n)	
livestock farming (n)	
manufacture (n)	
mining (n)	
primary (adj)	
provide (v)	
raw material (n)	
retail (n)	
secondary (adj)	
service (n)	
tertiary (adj)	

UNIT 6: Business and money

English	Your language	English	Your language
bank (n)	____________	expense (n)	____________
banknote (n)	____________	income (n)	____________
bartering (n)	____________	insurance (n)	____________
borrower (n)	____________	loan (n)	____________
business (n)	____________	loss (n)	____________
coin (n)	____________	microcredit (n)	____________
contract (v)	____________	money (n)	____________
cost (n)	____________	ongoing cost (n)	____________
currency (n)	____________	salary (n)	____________
development (n)	____________	staff (n)	____________
entrepreneur (v)	____________	value (n)	____________
exchange (v)	____________	variable (adj)	____________

Glossary

English	Your language	English	Your language

Unit 7: Modern Spain I

English	Your language	English	Your language
agreement (n)		lieutenant (n)	
alliance (n)		look for (v)	
border (n)		low-paid (adj)	
bourgeoisie (n)		machinery (n)	
coal (n)		manufacturing (n)	
cotton (n)		migrate (v)	
crown (v)		pollution (n)	
defeat (v)		railway (n)	
draw up (v)		regent (n)	
eldest (adj)		right (n)	
engine (n)		sign (v)	
exile (n)		steam-powered (adj)	
fabric (n)			
factory (n)		support (n)	
gap (n)		take place (v)	
heat (n)		thread (n)	
home life (n)		throne (n)	
horse-drawn barge (n)		unemployed (adj)	
		uprising (n)	
huge (adj)		wages (n)	
Industrial Revolution (n)		weaving (adj)	
		wheel (n)	
invest (v)		widen (v)	
landowner (n)		worker (n)	

English	Your language

Unit 8: Modern Spain II

English	Your language
ancient (adj)	
attempt (n)	
bankruptcy (n)	
beliefs (n)	
break out (v)	
Contemporary Age (n)	
cope (v)	
coup d'etat (n)	
current (adj)	
democracy (n)	
dictatorship (n)	
empire (n)	
eventually (adv)	
fight (v)	
force (n)	
fraud (n)	
gold (n)	
grandson (n)	
hardship (n)	
last (v)	
major (adj)	
minor (adj)	
oil producer (n)	
peace (n)	
political party (n)	
population (n)	
pressure (n)	
ration book (n)	
reign (n)	
release (n)	
repress (v)	
rule (n)	
self-sufficiency (n)	
silver (n)	
strike (n)	
take over (v)	
takeover (n)	
timeline (n)	
trade (n)	
trade union (n)	
troops (n)	
unrest (n)	
verge (n)	
weak (adj)	
weapon (n)	
withstand (v)	

Glossary

Unit 9: Spain today

English	Your language
achievement (n)	
ageing population (n)	
alive (adj)	
average (n)	
award (n)	
ballot paper (n)	
bicameral (adj)	
birth rate (n)	
boundary (n)	
budget (n)	
campaign (v)	
challenge (v)	
chamber (n)	
citizen (n)	
coat of arms (n)	
court (n)	
cyberbullying (n)	
dead (adj)	
disagreement (n)	
duty (n)	
envelope (n)	
environment (n)	
executive (adj)	

English	Your language
face (v)	
flag (n)	
freely (adv)	
Government (n)	
head of state (n)	
hereditary (adj)	
infographic (n)	
judge (n)	
judicial (adj)	
legislative (adj)	
life expectancy (n)	
low (adj)	
ministry (n)	
prime minister (n)	
race (n)	
reject (v)	
responsibility (n)	
restore (v)	
social networking (n)	
taxes (n)	
totalitarian (adj)	
veto (v)	